A note to parents, grandparents, teachers, and all others:

DISCOVER GRAND TETON is written for elementary school children. Light-hearted illustrations accompany the informative text as well as participatory activities which enhance creativity and learning for the reader.

Information about Grand Teton National Park includes: geology, flora and fauna study, history of the region, recreational activities, Park Ranger involvement, and preservation.

Written by Bobbi Salts
Illustrated by Steve Parker

Produced by American Educational Press
a division of Double B Publications
4113 N. Longview
Phoenix, Arizona 85014

ISBN # 0-931895-22-7
Printed in the United States of America
Copyright © 1992 by Grand Teton Natural History Association
Moose, Wyoming 83012
All rights reserved, including the right of reproduction in whole or in part in any form.

Discover Grand Teton

The Teton Range Today	4-5
Formation of the Teton Range	6-7
Glaciers	8-9
Early Mammals	10
Man in the Tetons	11
Pioneers and Ranching	12
Grand Teton National Park	13
Hiking	14-15
The Snake River	16-17
Life-Zones	18-19
Mammals	20-21
Moose	22
National Elk Refuge	23
Small Mammals	24-25
Birds	26-27
Wildflowers	28
Trees	29
Mountaineering	30
Ranger-led Activities	31
Answer Page	32

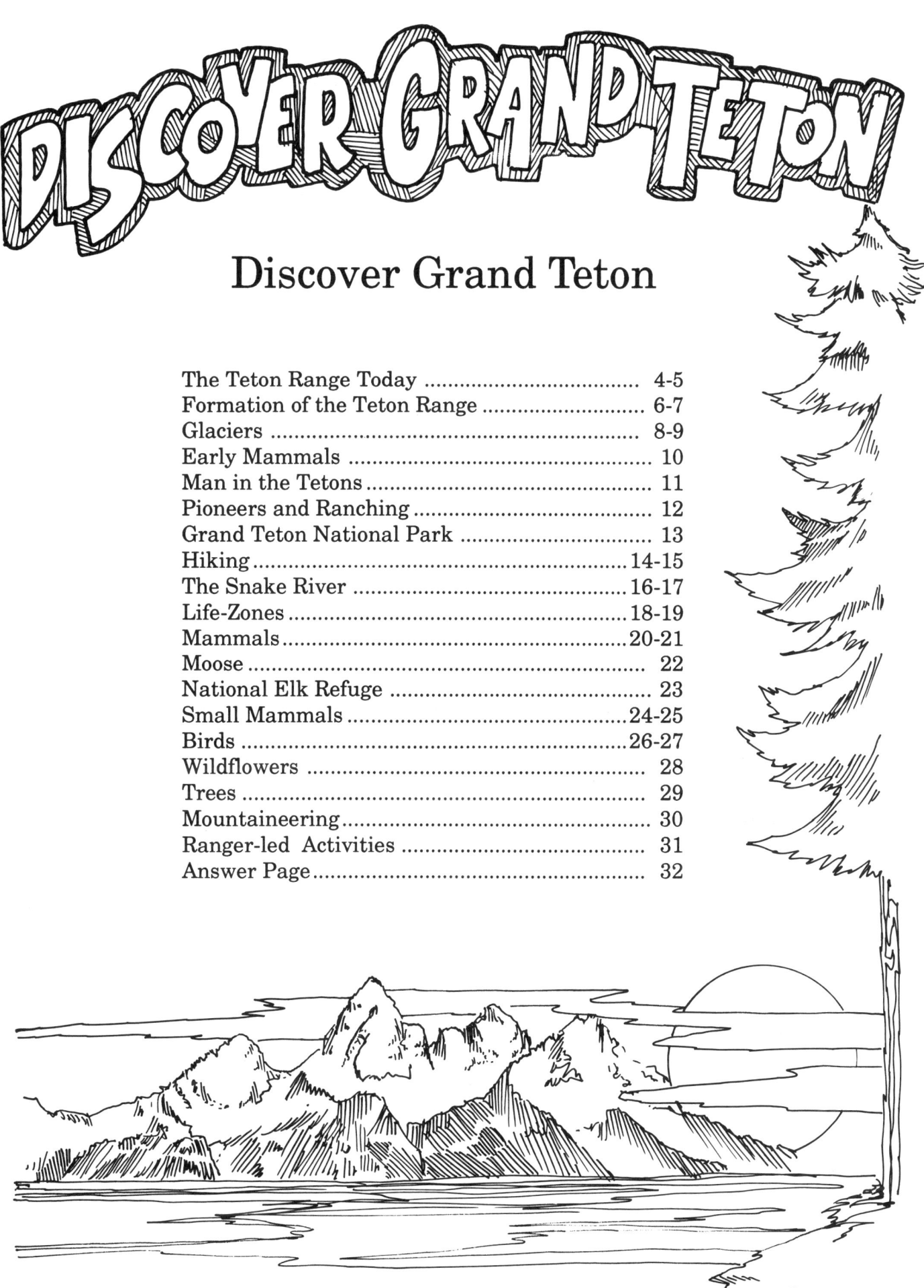

The Teton Range Today

The Teton Mountain Range is the youngest range in the Rocky Mountains to form. The mountains you see today have been shaped from uplift (lifting up), glaciers (moving ice), and erosion (wearing away by ice, water, wind, rain). This natural process of erosion and glaciers, which helped carve the mountains, is still happening today.

The mountains measure about 40 miles long and 10 to 15 miles wide. Lakes at the bottom of the mountains were formed from Ice Age glaciers many thousands of years ago.

The Snake River flows through the valley called Jackson Hole. The river comes from a mountain valley north of the Teton Range. The beautiful scenery, wildlife, and history complete the story of the Grand Teton National Park of today.

Formation of the Teton Range

The Teton Mountain Range first began to rise about ten million years ago. Before this time, ancient seas came and left and other mountains appeared and disappeared. About 80 million years ago, the Rocky Mountains were formed. The Teton Range is the youngest part of the Rocky Mountains to rise. Can you imagine such a long, long time ago?

Continual movement and pressure deep within the earth causes the earth's crust to crack along weak areas called **faults**. The crack, or fault, that occurred in Jackson Hole around 10 million years ago is called the Teton Fault. The Teton Fault separated the earth's crust into two part called the western and eastern blocks.

Pressure from the west caused the western block to rise while the pull of gravity caused the eastern block to sink. The Teton Mountain Range and Jackson Hole Valley were formed as a result of these natural forces.

An **avalanche** (snowslide) is another one of nature's most powerful forces. When snow slides or crashes down a mountainside, an avalanche is in progress. Most occur in rugged areas where they are not detected. Scientists believe that about 100,000 avalanches occur in North America each year and as many as a million happen throughout the world!

Avalanches begin in one of two ways: either as *loose snow* or as a *slab avalanche*. They may be wide or narrow. Avalanches may carry snow a few feet or down an entire mountainside.

Avalanche safety precautions are necessary to know if you plan to spend time in the mountains. Learn everything you can from an expert and check snow conditions before beginning a mountain trip. Avalanche danger is greater during, and immediately after, a heavy snowfall.

Glaciers

Glaciers (ice masses) form when snow accumulates faster than it melts during a season. The hardened snow turns to ice, and this ice begins to move downward from its own weight. Rocks which fall onto glaciers are carried along with the ice mass.

Can you imagine such masses causing the ragged ridges, sharp-pointed peaks, and U-shaped canyons of the Teton Range? Glaciers did most of the carving and shaping during the Ice Age. Today, small glaciers are found in shaded corners of the highest peaks such as the **Teton Glacier** and **Schoolroom Glacier.**

The Teton Glacier is believed to move nearly 30 feet a year. Ancient glaciers were much wider and deeper, similar to the larger Alaskan glaciers seen today. Ancient glaciers moved several hundred feet each year!

The upper part of a valley shaped by a glacier is called a **cirque** (deep hollow). The thickest part of the glacier carves the walls of the cirque. The glacier also scoops out a bowl-shaped area in the floor of the cirque. Melted ice may remain and form a lake within this bowl. **Amphitheater Lake, Lake Solitude,** and **Holly Lake** are a result of this process.

When glaciers melt and retreat, piles of rock and soil remain. The ridges at the glacier's end are called **terminal moraines** (glacial earth deposit). Melting also causes streams of water to pour from the end of the glacier. These streams carry material such as sand, gravel, and silt. This material is called **outwash** and the area in front of the glacier is called the **outwash plain**.

Some of the glaciers left behind blocks of ice. Soil flowed around the ice block, building up the land around the ice block. When the ice block melted, a large depression remained. The large depressions are called **kettles** or **potholes**. Water has filled many of the kettles, providing areas for water and nesting for wildlife.

The diagram below illustrates the carving effect of glaciers.

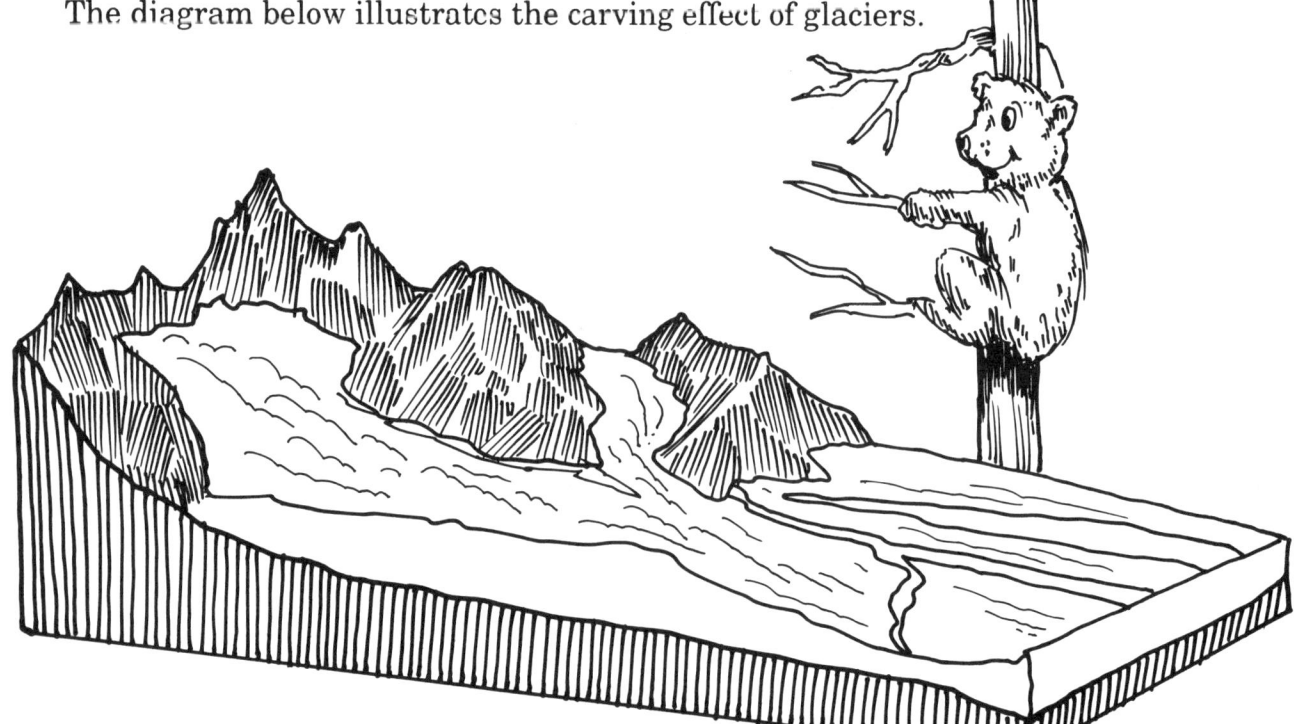

GLACIER WORD SEARCH

See if you can discover the words in the glacier word search below. They are all the new words you just learned relating to glaciers. The words can be horizontal, vertical, forward, and backward. Check your answers with those located on the answer page.

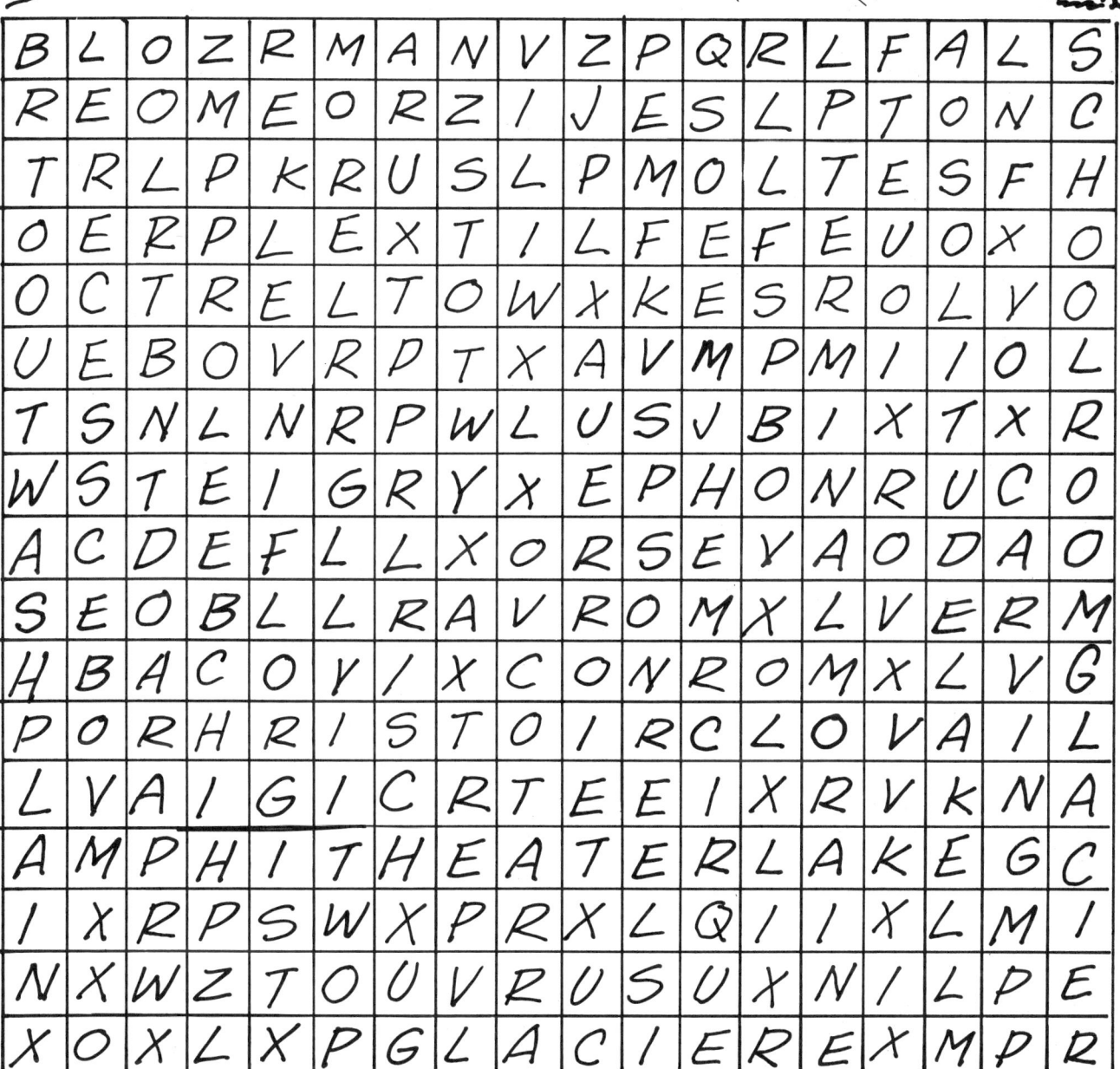

FIND THESE WORDS!

GLACIER
TETON GLACIER
SCHOOLROOM GLACIER
CIRQUE
AMPHITHEATER LAKE
SOLITUDE LAKE
HOLLY LAKE
TERMINAL MORAINE
OUTWASH
OUTWASH PLAIN
RECESS
CARVING
KETTLES
MOLT

Early Mammals

During the "Age of Mammals," about 65 million years ago, the sub-tropical, humid climate was much different than it is today. Swamps, lakes, and rivers covered much of the land which was nearly at sea level. Many kinds of plant life such as grasses, tropical breadfruits, figs, and flowers dotted the landscape. Trees such as maple, oak, hickory, and redwood shaded the ground. Gar fish and crocodiles were found in streams. Dog-sized horses and other small mammals roamed the plains. The **environment** (surroundings) provided favorable conditions for survival and mammals thrived and multiplied.

Examples include the **Titanotheres** (a large four-legged mammal the size of a rhinoceros), which lived in the area for a few million years and then disappeared. Small camels, some pig-like animals, and saber-toothed tigers (**Machaeroides**) roamed the area as well.

There are 10 differences in these two pictures. Can you find them all?

Man In The Tetons

For thousands of years Native Americans hunted wildlife and gathered plants in the Tetons, but the harsh winters prevented most of them from staying all year. In the 1800's, a small group of Shoshone people camped in the Tetons for as many months as they could. The Shoshone depended upon the bighorn sheep for their food and they were called the Sheep Eaters. The Sheep Eaters lived in small family units until they joined Chief Washakie of the Eastern Shoshone. Today, Shoshone artifacts and much more can be seen at the Colter Bay Indian Arts Museum. The museum houses the treasures of David T. Vernon, Indian art collector.

John Colter is believed to be the first non-Indian to visit Jackson Hole. He crossed the valley in the winter of 1807-08. Mountain men like Jedediah Smith, David Jackson, Jim Bridger, and others came to trap beaver. After the fur trade stopped, a few prospectors and trappers wandered into the valley, but did not stay. A valley was called a "hole" by trappers and the most popular one is Jackson Hole, named for the mountain man David Jackson.

Indians painted stories about their life experiences on animal hides and teepees. You can tell others about your life, too. Create your own symbols and record your story below.

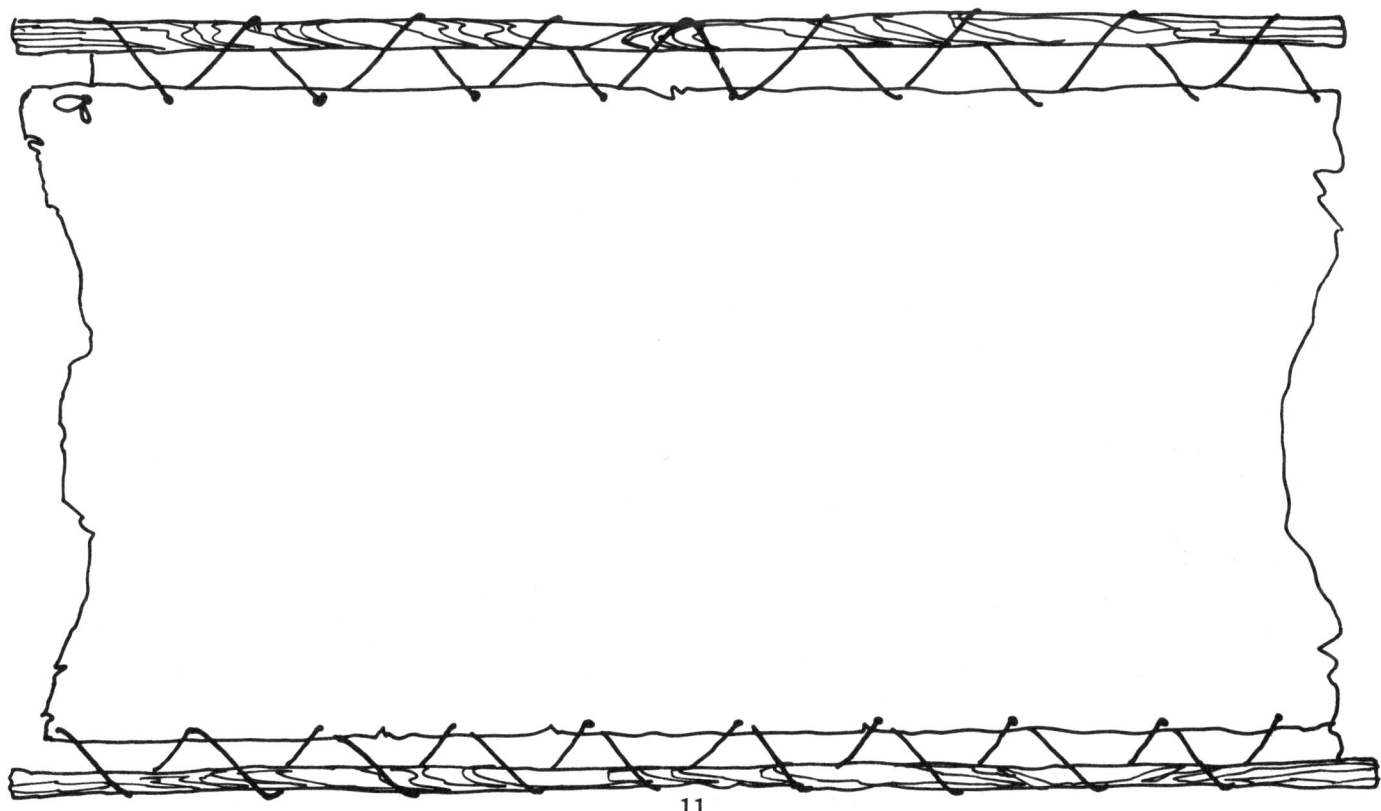

Pioneers and Ranching

John Holland and John Carnes were the first permanent settlers in Jackson Hole in 1884. Others followed and ranching became the chief livelihood for the homesteaders. After 1900, many communities such as Jackson, Kelly, Moran, and Wilson were founded. When ranchers realized the beautiful scenery and magnificent wildlife were a special natural resource, some opened dude ranches and hunting lodges. The business of tourism began and is very popular today.

You can visit the Cunningham Cabin and the Joe Pfeiffer Homestead. The Cunningham's two-room homestead is built with logs and a sod roof. Can you imagine living in a homestead, similar to the Cunningham Cabin, during the harsh winter season?

The items illustrated below were common among pioneers. Match the item with its definition. Draw a line from the picture to the letter that describes the item.

(butter churn, powder horn, spinning wheel, candle lantern, wheat cradle, snowshoes)

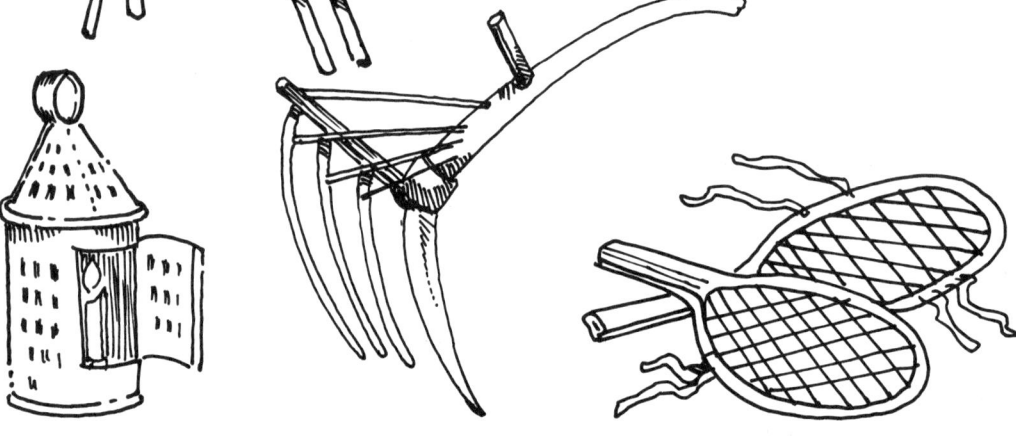

A. Made from an animal and used to carry gunpowder.

B. Early lighting gadget.

C. Used for making thread or yarn.

D. A device used to make butter from milk or cream.

E. An early farming necessity used to harvest the crops.

F. A strapped frame used for walking in deep snow.

Grand Teton National Park

Many local residents of Jackson Hole, including the Superintendent of Yellowstone National Park, Mr. Horace Albright, met at Maude Noble's Cabin in 1923. The concerned citizens gathered to discuss a plan to set aside a portion of Jackson Hole as a recreation area. This plan would prevent commercial development of the land and would guarantee protection and preservation of all the wildlife living there.

Although many people were against this plan, Congress voted in 1929 to create Grand Teton National Park. The original boundaries of 150 square miles included just the mountain range and lakes. The valley would not be protected under these conditions.

However, Congress passed a new law in 1950. Now, Grand Teton National Park includes the old park, the Grand Teton National Monument formed in 1943, and lands donated by a generous gentleman, John D. Rockefeller, Jr.

The wonderful natural resources of Grand Teton National Park are now protected and preserved for you and everyone, especially future generations.

Hiking

Have you ever seen a moose or a pronghorn in their natural surroundings as you hiked? You may, perhaps, catch a glimpse of these and other wild creatures. Look closely, for some of the best scenery is reserved for hikers.

Self-guided, short-to-medium hikes on established trails explore the nature and history of Jackson Hole. Information about these trails is provided at visitor centers or at trailheads. Menor's Ferry Historic Trail, Cascade Canyon Trail, Cunningham Cabin Trail, Taggart Lake Trail, Colter Bay Trail, and Lunch Tree Hill Trail are all self-guided hiking trails that are perfect for family or group outings.

Rangers will help guide you to the trail best suited for your abilities. Remember to be prepared. Wear comfortable and sturdy footgear. Carry rainwear (thunderstorms are common and often happen suddenly). Carry plenty of water taken from approved public supplies because sunny and hot conditions produce thirsty hikers! High energy snacks, light lunch, hat, sunscreen, and a camera should complete your pack.

Choose a marker. Flip a coin for moves:
heads—move one space, tails—move two spaces.

You can experience some of the most spectacular wilderness when you hike in the backcountry of the Tetons. You must keep in mind some **"backcountry basics"** to follow before you begin your adventure.

You must have a free *backcountry use permit* for any overnight backcountry stay. Wilderness experiences are desired by a great many people, so be sure to reserve your permit 24 hours in advance.

Can you imagine seeing a bear in the wilderness? Black bears are sometimes seen in the backcountry. Bears are not afraid of people and may even try to steal your food. Be sure to follow Park regulations about storing and hanging food. Do not approach bears or any other wild animal. Report any bear sighting to a park ranger. Informational brochures about bears are available at ranger stations and you will want to get one before you depart.

The Snake River

Do you know where the Snake River comes from? It starts its journey from the mountains north of Jackson Hole near Yellowstone National Park. It flows for 1,000 miles from its origin to the Columbia River near Pasco, Washington. Only forty miles of the twisting river is located in Jackson Hole, but the wildlife of the region is very dependent upon the river. Do you know why?

The river community is quite special. Vegetation, insects, fish, birds, and mammals are linked together for survival since one depends upon another for food. This is called a **food chain** and each living thing is an important link in it. Without one of these links, the rest of the chain would have difficulty surviving.

For example, the native Snake River cutthroat trout depends upon water insects, small fish, and **invertebrates** (animals with no backbone) for survival. Animals such as ospreys, eagles, bears, and otters depend upon trout for their survival. If the trout population decreases, perhaps due to overfishing by humans, the wildlife of the park could be in danger. Do you see then how each link in the food chain depends upon the other for survival?

There are many exciting activities centered around the Snake River. Canoeing, boating, and rafting are common ways to experience a river adventure. Mornings and evenings are the best times for observing wildlife. You may see a moose along the banks, bald eagles soaring high in the sky, or beavers, otters, and ducks diving into the water. The river view is one of the best ways to observe the beauty of Grand Teton National Park. What other wildlife might you see?

Fishing is also a very popular activity. Any angler will want to share his excitement with you as he catches a fish or two! Fishing is regulated and licenses are required, so be sure to check with a park ranger for important guidelines.

Life Zones

When you explore Grand Teton National Park, you will notice many varieties of plants and animals. You will discover that various plants and animals live in different places. You will also notice changes in the climate in different areas. These differences are due to changes in elevation. Every thousand foot change in elevation brings a change in rainfall and temperature. Scientists call this thinking the "life zone" theory and the different environments are called **life zones**.

Plants have learned to adapt to changing environments. When several kinds of plants grow within a similar environment, it is called a plant community. Animals live in the plant community in which they can best survive and they obtain food and shelter there. Some animals can live in more than one community, but others cannot. Do you know which animal can live in all zones, in all communities? Look in a mirror to find the answer!

Grand Teton National Park has ten major plant communities. This explains why there is so much wildlife in the Tetons.

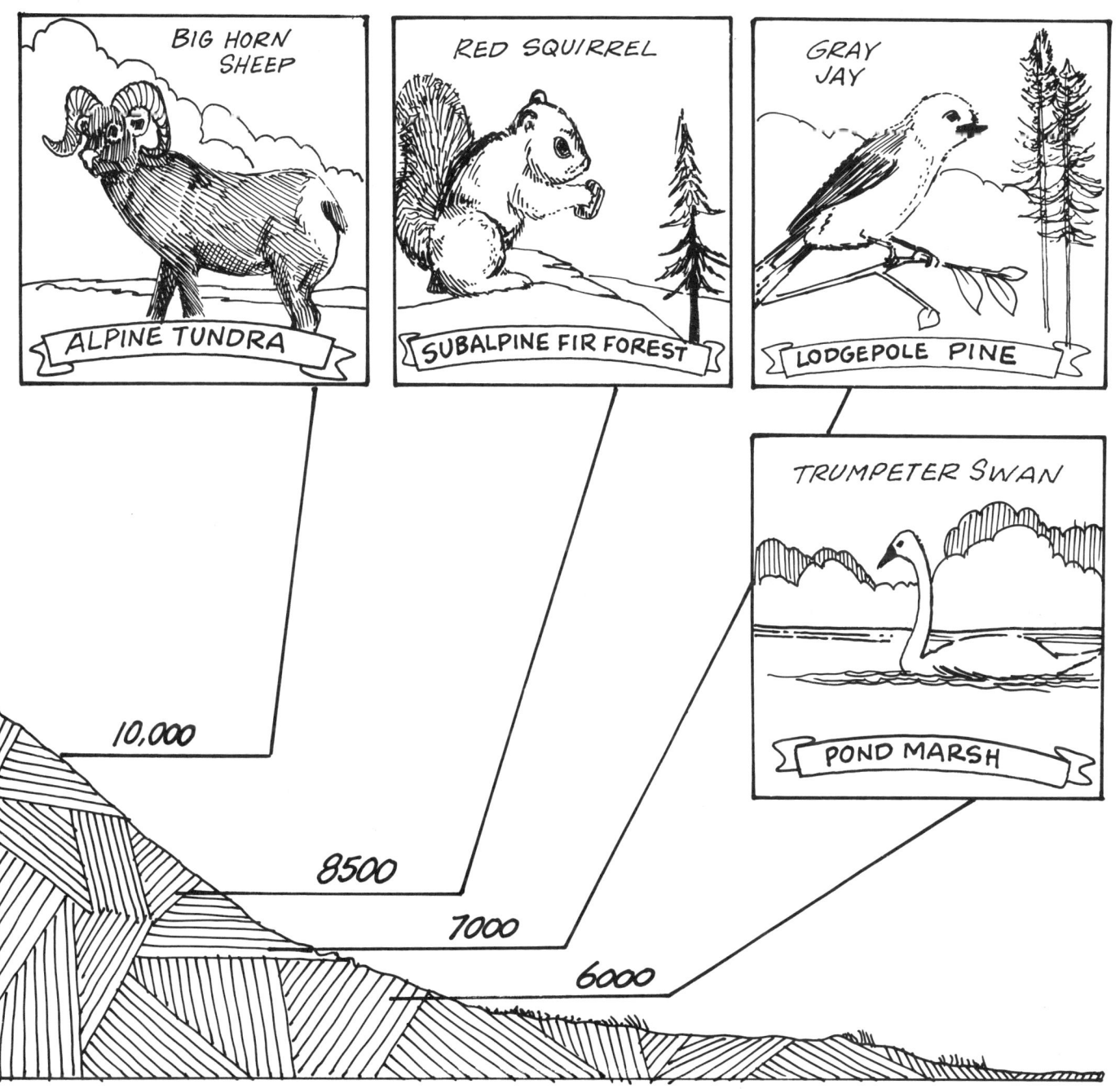

Mammals

Mammals are warm-blooded animals which grow hair, have a backbone, and provide milk for their young. There are many varieties of mammals within Grand Teton National Park. Visitors may see many of the following creatures along short hikes in the backcountry or even along the roadside. You should never attempt to approach any wild animal or feed one (it is illegal). Feeding will harm the wildlife and animals must find their own food in order to survive in their natural environment.

Identify each of the following animals to find the answers to the crossword puzzle on the next page. Clues are given for each animal. Check your answers with those located on the answer page.

Down:

1. The largest and most powerful member of the deer family. Its favorite food is marsh plants and it wades in swamps and ponds to reach them.

2. The largest mammal in North America. Man almost caused them to become extinct from needless killing. Likes to graze on prairie grasses and travels in large herds.

3. Mother is very aggressive when protecting young. Can climb trees to safety. Black, brown, cinnamon, and blond in color. Sleeps during winter months.

4. Often seen at dusk searching for food. They have large ears and are very swift and graceful.

5. Has large, curled horns. At home on high, rocky slopes and tundra areas during summer months. Retreats to lower elevations in winter. Hooves are curved inward on the bottom like suction cups.

Across:

1. Known for its howls, yips, and wails. This animal resembles a dog and is very intelligent. Seldom seen for more than a few seconds.

2. Makes a loud, bugling sound during mating season. Sometimes called Wapiti. Migrates to special refuge in winter.

3. Member of the rodent family. Has large, gnawing teeth to cut down trees. Builds dams of sticks, mud, and gravel.

4. Known as an antelope. Also known to be the fastest land animal in America. Can sprint 40-50 miles per hour. Males (bucks) shed their horns in late winter.

Moose

The Shiras moose, the largest and mightiest member of the deer family, has lived in Grand Teton for about 150 years. It can be seen wading in ponds and marshes feeding on lily pads and other water plants. Aspen and willow are popular winter meals. The male (bull) moose engages in fierce battles over females (cows) during the mating season (September and October) and clashing sounds of locking antlers can be heard throughout the park.

The moose has humped shoulders and a **dewlap** (fold of skin) hanging from its neck. Each year, the bull moose sheds its antlers in winter and by mid-summer a new set will have grown. The new antlers have a soft, velvety covering which is rubbed off, often against a tree trunk, by the bull. The antlers become shiny and hard once again in time for mating season.

National Elk Refuge

Elk can be seen migrating south during the month of November. Winter snows force the elk from their summer home in high mountain meadows down to the valley. The elk sometimes travel about 70 miles to the National Elk Refuge at the south end of the Park near the town of Jackson. What an exciting experience to witness!

First established in 1912 by concerned citizens, the Refuge is managed by the U.S. Fish and Wildlife Service. Today, about 7,500 elk make the Refuge their winter home. When snows become so deep that the elk cannot secure their own food supply, alfalfa pellets are provided by National Elk Refuge managers. The elk remain on the Refuge for about six months before migrating north again in the spring.

Can you find your way down from the mountain meadows?

Small Mammals

Small mammals are found throughout the Park. See if you can spot some of the most common small mammals where you explore. Don't get too close!

Uinta Ground Squirrel—This animal **hibernates** (sleeps in winter) underground until March or April. Its food consists of dandelions, grasses, seeds, roots, and leaves. Its young are born in May. When the heat of summer begins, it may return to burrow for **estivation** (summer hibernation). Uinta ground squirrels can go from summer to winter hibernation and remain underground for eight to nine months!

Marmot—Lush mountain meadows which contain rockslides and boulders are homes for marmots. They build underground dens and eat alpine grasses and wildflowers. The marmot hibernates in winter. A litter of four to six will be born in March.

Pika—Another name for this animal is "rock rabbit" because it is related to rabbits. Winter meals consist of grasses and plants cut and stored during the summer. These six-inch creatures are quite shy and stay out of sight as much as possible.

Least Chipmunk—Dry grass meadows are favorite feeding grounds for the least chipmunk. Its lifestyle is a cross between a tree and ground squirrel and it eats seeds and berries.

Striped Skunk—This unique animal has strong-smelling musk glands. It sprays a stinky smelling musk into an enemy's eyes up to ten feet away! The skunk prefers the sagebrush-grassland areas to hunt mice, bird eggs, insects, and **carrion** (dead animals).

River Otter—Lakes and streams are home for this water animal. It builds an underwater den which has entrances from above or below water level. Two to three young are born in April and hunt for fish with their mother at about three months old.

Muskrat—This large rat lives in lowland marshes and slow-running streams. It eats water plants such as sedges, cattails, smartweeds, and rushes. Underground bank dens are its home and a new litter of five to six young are born in the summer.

Snowshoe Hare—This mammal lives in forests. It eats huckleberries and clover. During summer it is dull gray, blending in with the forest environment. In winter, it changes to white except for a small area on its ears. Hairs on its back legs grow longer to provide "snowshoes" for winter survival.

Porcupine—Sharp quills arm this mammal and protect it from its enemies. The quills are about four inches long on its back and about one inch long on its head. It is very unsociable and prefers to be alone as it moves about meadows and forests. The porcupine eats the bark from trees and can harm or kill a tree if too much of the bark is stripped away.

Birds

An area in which a plant or animal lives is called a **habitat**. Birds of Grand Teton live in many different habitats. Nest sites, food, shelter, and water are needed for survival. Birds may stay in one habitat or visit others. The habitats include: sagebrush flats, forests, water (river, lakes, ponds) and alpine.

Watching birds in their natural habitat is a great experience and lots of fun. To be a responsible "birder" you must keep in mind that nesting birds can be disturbed very easily. If a bird flies in circles above you, screams in alarm, or flies from the nest when you approach, you have come too close! Back away immediately, for babies will not survive if left alone for very long!

Bald eagles, trumpeter swans, ospreys, sage grouse, ruffed grouse, mountain bluebirds, and gray jays are some of the common birds living in the Tetons.

Wildflowers

If you visit Grand Teton during the summer, you will discover colorful carpets of wildflowers that spread across the valley, mountainsides, and meadows. The summer season comes late and the flowers usually bloom for just a short time.

Wildflowers depend upon birds, insects, mammals, water, and wind for survival. In return, the flower provides food (nectar and pollen) for animals and insects. Flowers display their best colors and scents to attract visitors such as these.

Balsamroot, lupine, and fireweed are a few of the common flowers you will notice. You can capture their beauty in a photograph, but remember not to pick any flowers. They should be left for others to enjoy, too.

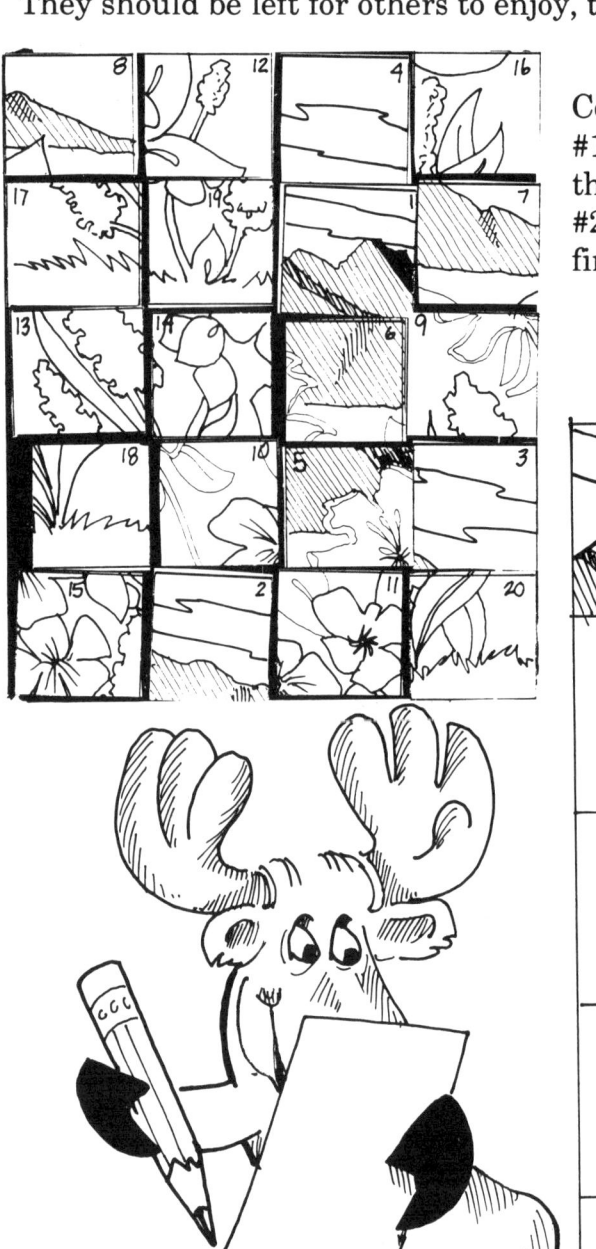

Complete the mystery picture below. Find square #1 in the jumbled picture. See how it is drawn in the square below. Now it is your turn. Find square #2 and copy what you see. Complete each square to finish your picture.

Trees

As you explore Grand Teton National Park, you will discover that trees live within different zones. Some of the more common trees include the aspen, lodgepole pine, Engelmann spruce, cottonwood, and Douglas fir. As with other wildlife, trees have special conditions best suited for survival. Some prefer sunny, dry locations, while others prefer north-facing, cool, moist slopes.

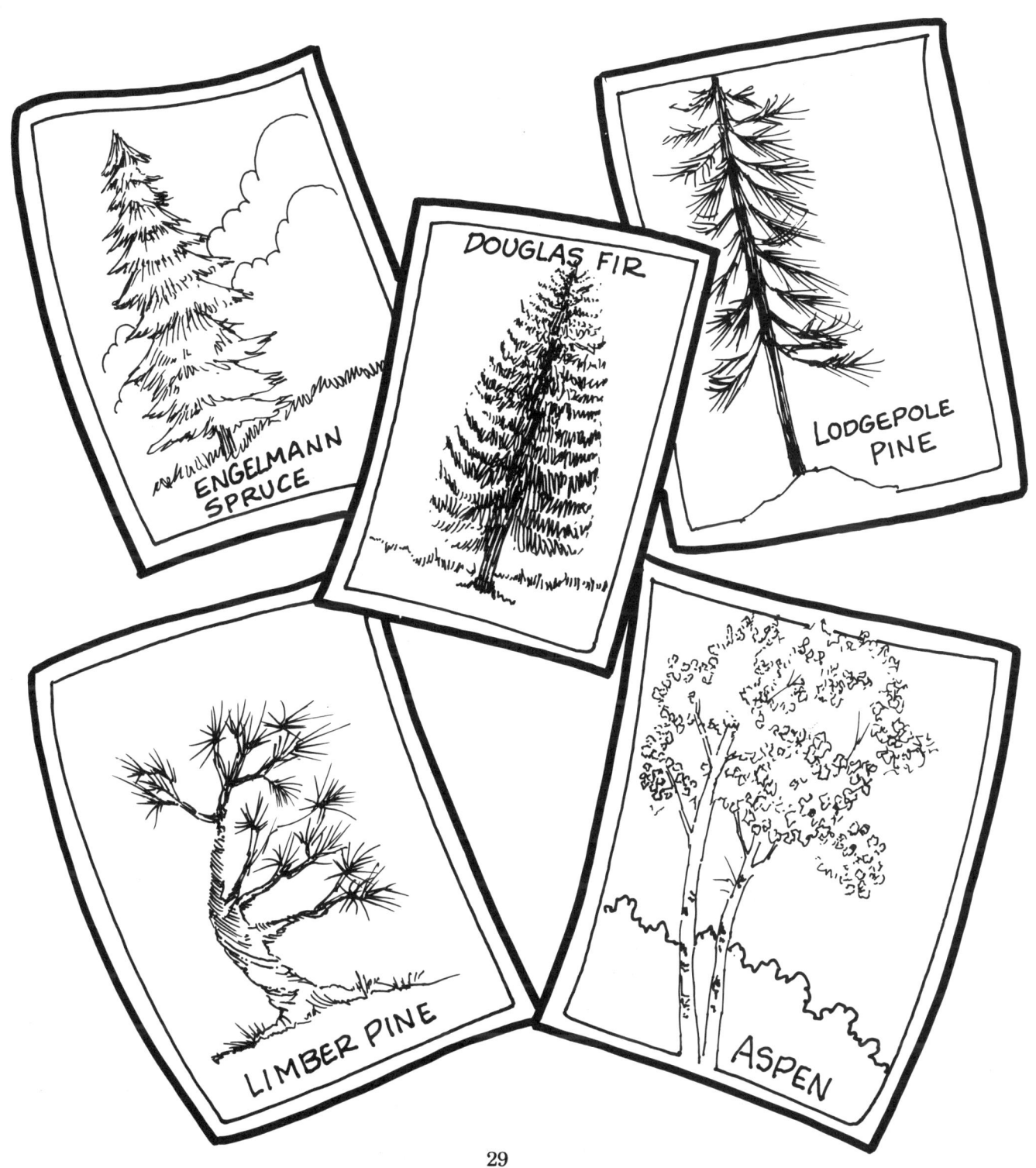

Mountaineering

The hard granite rock, ice, snow, and beautiful scenery of the Teton Mountains make this area a very popular destination for **mountaineers** (mountain climbers). Cracks and ledges are plentiful, providing hand and foot holds so important for the **ascent** (climb up). The mountains are easy to get to and there are many trails which offer a variety of levels of difficulty. This is why many mountain climbers choose the Tetons for their adventures. However, mountaineers must be aware of rapidly-changing weather which can create unsafe conditions.

The National Park Service requires all climbers to check in before and after their climbs. Park Rangers provide important information about current conditions, trails, and equipment. Can you imagine being a mountain climber?

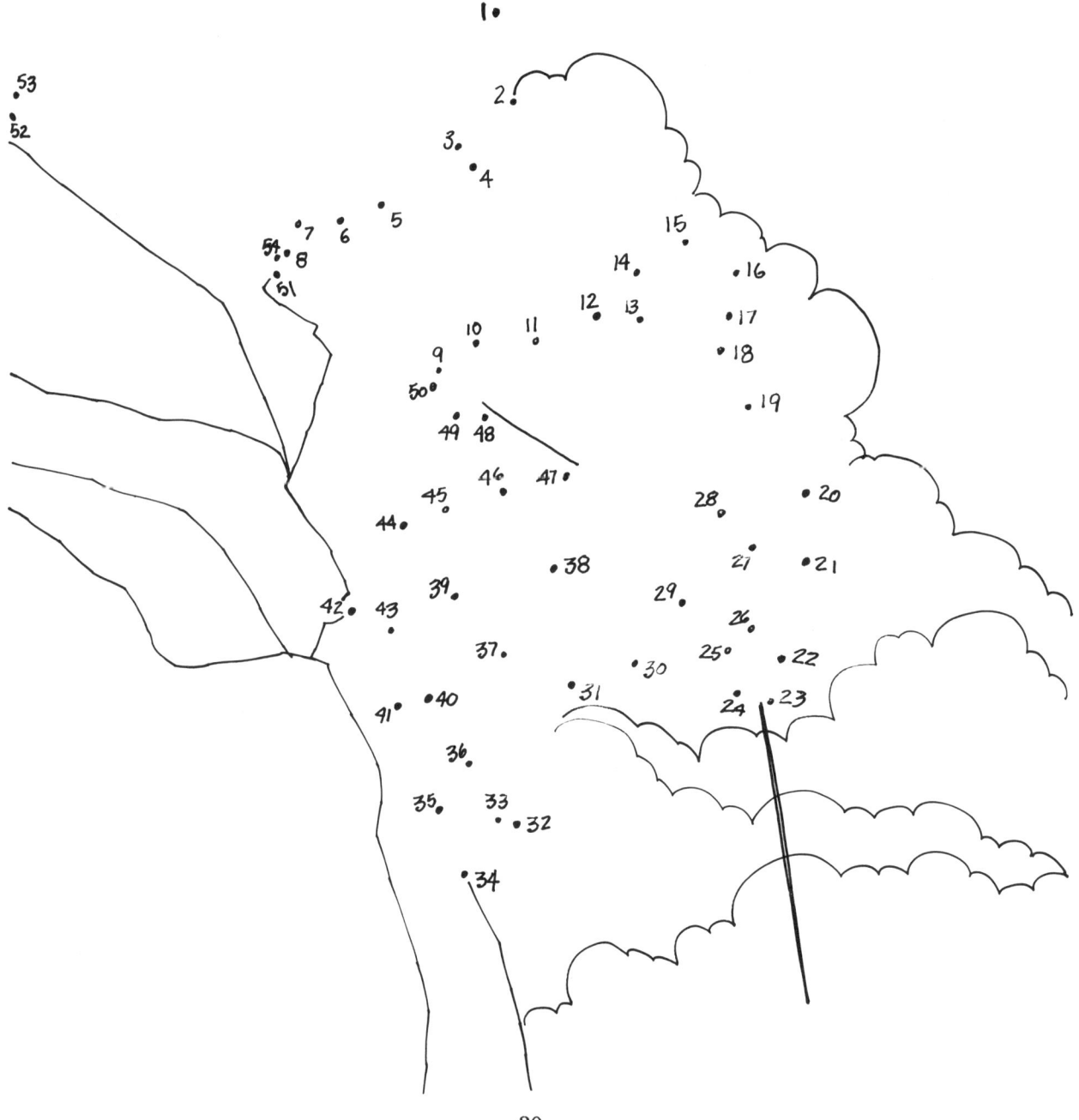

Ranger-led Activities

Do you know why it is important to have National Parks and Park Rangers?

National Parks are set aside by our government to protect and preserve the scenery, natural and historic objects, and wildlife found within parks. Each park is to be left undisturbed so future generations will continue to enjoy them. Park Rangers help you see, understand, and learn about the wondrous resources found in the park. They show you ways to preserve these precious resources for our future.

Ranger-led activities occur from mid-June through Labor Day. Some of these include hikes along mountain trails, park wildlife demonstrations, and campfire programs. Rangers have a great deal of knowledge they will enjoy sharing with you. Take advantage of these opportunities, if at all possible. You will want to check the schedule of events in the park newspaper, at the visitor centers, or in campgrounds.

Answer Page

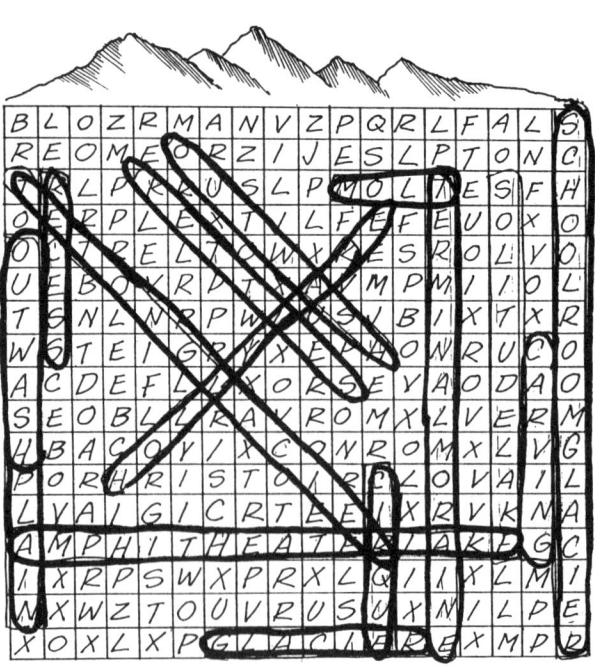

(butter churn, powder horn, spinning wheel, candle lantern, wheat cradle, snowshoes)

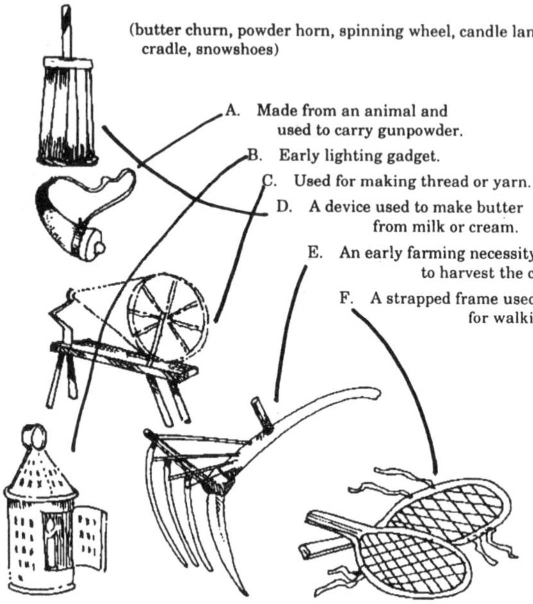

A. Made from an animal and used to carry gunpowder.
B. Early lighting gadget.
C. Used for making thread or yarn.
D. A device used to make butter from milk or cream.
E. An early farming necessity used to harvest the crops.
F. A strapped frame used for walking in deep snow.

ANIMAL CROSSWORD

GRAND TETON NATIONAL PARK FOR PRESENT AND FUTURE GENERATIONS!

There are 10 differences in these two pictures. Can you find them all!?

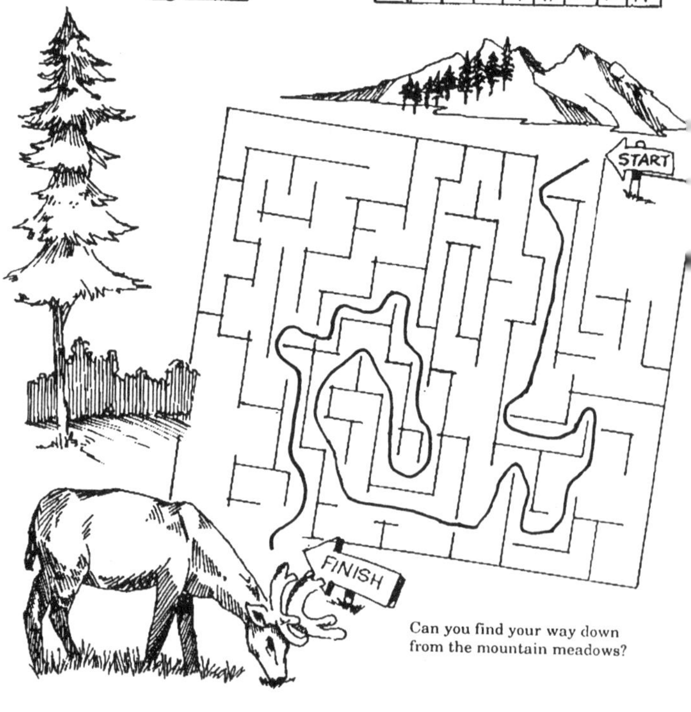

Can you find your way down from the mountain meadows?